the lovers' tree

you know this tree
the one in the cemetery

by the lake where cattails
grow straight, poking their heads
through amniotic water
while bodies, epitaphs fade

you've seen it
stretch its long fingertips
its trunk the shared leg
of ten contortionists backbending
boneless in the wind
grazing a strand of hair, tickling an arm
pushing lovers

together
its roots trip sweethearts
falling into each other's embrace

when this tree blooms in Spring
shade and a private place
bring stolen kisses and confessions

i often see you there
but shadows distort
your face

in Fall, its tears sprinkle the ground with gold
as its last lovers
of the year mark its bark

we were them
once, you crouched down
found an empty spot
i handed you the knife

in Winter i am the only visitor
i see straight through its bare
loveless branches
my ghostlike breaths trapped
with the stars

its stripped form offers me nothing—
an unobstructed view
to the opposite shore
where moonlight drips
on graves, your
grave

i will return
in Spring

the lovers' tree

lucia snyderman

the lovers' tree

"those who dwell among the beauties and mysteries

of the Earth are never alone or weary of life"

— rachel carson

acknowledgements

a special thanks to the following people:
my family
my friends
Leah Brennan
Joshua Smith
Anna Redcay
Antonia Losano
Stacie Cassarino

thank you all for believing in me and inspiring me
to write!

instagram: thepittsburghpoet
email: snyderman.lucia@gmail.com

i will watch the lovers return
to our tree

the roots

what is love

rose lenses
allowing lovers to see

buds sighing a breath of spring
petals open to blooming
sunrises and dewy days

as we surrender dandelion puffs
wind's tongue flicks wishes
like shooting star tails

a golden sun on a chain
glowing against my neck

our hands intertwined, caught
in a web of sweat and scented lotion

my arms the gutters
to hold your rain, love

fleeting as Cupid's wings
inside a heart take flight

flames waltzing cheek to cheek
lips part for air, feeding the fire

tilt of a head and closed eyes
nose bumps, a nervous laugh

a doll's heart

a flick of a brush splatters
sparkles on Barbie's platinum hair

dangling upside down, smiling
bare foot hooked onto my finger

she faceplants in the winter snow
eyelashes frozen, eyes unblinking

i stand tall, mimicking her perfect posture
resilience through wind, sleet, snow

that kind of strength comes
with a frostbitten heart of gold

the one who forgot how to live

she was a mountain
her face a marble slate

but they didn't see
when it rained
she lost a part of herself

it took years of tears
to erode a mountain
to a pebble

it took years of sitting in the past
for the butterfly to forget
how to fly

time was all she had
so she climbed back into her cocoon

where the world forgot her
but she remembered the world

solitude

she was a flower that never bloomed
knew only darkness

the sun was something she dreamt
a figment of her imagination

so she stayed
in her corner of the world

afraid to unfold her petals
to surrender herself to the scrutiny
of sun's harsh glare

ocean eyes

i still see him the same
after the storm

summoned from the ocean
in his eyes

rainclouds trampled the sun
but light pierced darkness

ocean replaced
with a cloudless sky

the storm is retreating
from my mind

i must have dreamt it all

but i still taste salt
from tears crashing
in waves against my soul

volcano mind

in that moment
her volcano mind erupted

why then?
she didn't know

memories of him
resurfaced like lava
gushing from head to heart

what her heart knew as love
her head failed to recognize

and so she turned into ash
slipping through hands
hopelessly grasping for her

stood up at the Grand Lux Cafe

between bites of red velvet pancakes
and sugar-dusted beignets

i saw a woman by the window
looking out, expecting
someone

when the waiter came by
pen in hand, ready to take orders
he didn't notice her

only i saw her

she turned her head, smiled
at me like i was more
than a stranger

who was she
and more importantly
who was i

were we lovers, friends, family?
no

we were two ghosts from the past
seated in the present
stood up by life

frozen

if i could do it all over again
i would in a heartbeat

even if it means i have to lose you twice

those moments, a flicker in time
were worth the pain

i'm glad it was you
and i would never wish to forget
the way you, only you, made me feel

if i had you at one point in time
maybe, just maybe, i can redirect you
back into the past

throw fate off your track
and you will find me

where i've always been
frozen in time

who am i

i am the sun
you see me, i see you

but with a breath, you freckle
a touch, you burn

i am the stars
you see me
silently blinking outside
your bedroom window

i see you close the drapes at night
i find company with the moon
an eclipsed version of you

i am the wind
you feel me, i feel you

my boneless fingers try to find holes
in the scarf you knit last winter
to keep me out
my cold from your warm

i am the rain
you feel your tears merge with my own
i feel the lips i used to kiss

you hide under an umbrella
letting me fall past, a puddle
at your heel

i am everywhere
you are

what now

my heart says *stay and fight*
my head says *move on*

my friends say *just be friends*
my family says *there are plenty of fish in the sea*

but how can they speak for me
without carrying my heart
my memories of you

once i think you've slipped my mind
the universe punishes me

i replay the moment your hand fit into mine
when you hugged me in front of all your friends
kissed me for the first time behind bookshelves

i pray to God and Aphrodite and Grandpa in heaven
anyone who might hear me

i ask for a sign, anything

do i trust that if it's meant to be, it'll happen?
or do i fight and be saved from regret
for all the things i could've said and done?

how can we be friends
if it's torture to be with you
but not truly with you

there may be plenty of fish in the sea
but you are the ocean to me

seamless love

i see him everywhere

in my dreams
in strangers' faces on the street

but i found a new love
a seamless love

places and objects cannot hurt me
the way people do

so i go to the ocean
surfboard in hand
to ride the waves
that crash, pull me down

unlike him, these waves
allow me to resurface

unlike him, they do not lie
they do not pretend

i know the ocean's power
from the moment i step foot
on its saturated sand

we have an understanding
of one another

the ocean has taught me
i don't need him
just as the ocean belongs to no one

push

i push, and push, and push
people away

so i won't feel
the rush of my heart beating
again

because the last person drained me
of logic and wisdom

implanted a blind faith
to love without reason

i push, and push, and push
people away

and yet i hope they stay
look into my eyes and know
i don't mean what i say

but the good ones and the bad ones
they all walk away

a little nudge, a little shove
that's all it takes
to throw my love away

end of the wick

that beautiful light in the sky
slow-roasting the planet and us
will burn out as all things do

nothing is infinite

there are pale green moths
with white eye spots on velvet wings
and no mouth
that live for a week

time is borrowed for you and me

we are only as strong as the wick of a candle
burning closer and closer to the puddle of wax

nothing beautiful

there's nothing beautiful
about lighting yourself on fire
to keep someone warm

there's nothing beautiful
about the way he led her on
to believe that he was the one

there's nothing beautiful
about living one chapter of a fairytale
to be ripped out of the pages

but

there's something beautiful
about the way she saved herself

how she built a ship
to sail the ocean of her tears

something beautiful

there's something beautiful
about lighting oneself on fire
to keep someone warm

there's something beautiful about broken glass
how it cuts the world into pieces

there's something beautiful about how tears run
from the corner of an eye to a mouth
so sadness can be tasted in two places at once

there's something beautiful
about wishing on a dandelion
blowing the fairy seeds to the wind

we don't have to look too far

let's find something beautiful
in ourselves

jump

my friend told me there's a door to the roof
three floors up

there's a chain on the door
but the door's unlocked

it's quiet up here, she said
looking over the edge at the ground below

no one noticed her up there
no one noticed her anywhere

what would happen if i jumped?
she asked

would anyone care?
i told her i would
care

but she didn't hear me

i've always wanted to fly
maybe it's time i tried
and it's ok if i fall
at least i'll know i tried

that was the last thing she said

oasis

she was a ghost
flickering like a dying flame

her words suspended in clouds
evaporated before heard

she found a friend in the moon
waning in pale comparison to the sun

she said to the moon:
don't despair for you have the light of stars
to guide you through darkness

i am an oasis
you think you can reach me

but with every step
i recede
further into the past

not human

they were barked at
herded like sheep

dogs snapped at their heels
with teeth made of whips and rocks

this breed could stand on two legs
and tore mothers from their babies

husbands were locked in crates
eyes peering out on an open slaughterhouse

gold on molars plucked, hair sheared
names replaced with numbers

a fate worse awaited

families that made it to safety
asked about their loved ones
but the names they spoke
were the words of a dead language

shapeshifter

it flows in my blood like a fish
swimming against the tide

other days it sits on my shoulder like a bird
whispering into my ear things i'm too scared
to admit

it's the sweat on my hands when i'm talking to
someone
it's the needles pinning the corners of my mouth
into a smile

it looks through my eyes distorting what i see
it makes me question
who i am, what i am, why i am

it's everywhere and nowhere
it goes to bed with me every night

it wakes up with me every morning
asking the same question: why?

i'm afraid one day i won't have an answer
and i won't
get up

the night we met

i remember the night we met
a few days after Valentine's day

i felt your warmth across the crowded room
and closed the distance

i challenged you to a game
you let me win

i remember the first time we held hands
at an 80's themed dance

i wore hoop earrings
and a sunflower skirt

you made me a glow-stick bracelet
with two lollipops in your mouth

i reached for your hand
and you weaved your sticky fingers
through my Cheeto-dusted ones

i remember the first time we kissed
behind my mom's car

you asked if you could kiss me goodnight
and i pulled you into shadow

i let you into my house
and months later, i still see you there

i'll find myself staring at the wall
where you grabbed me by the waist
held me tight

or the cushion on my couch
you lay your arm on
while i curled up next to you

i remember looking at you across restaurant tables
smiling when you ordered the same thing

i remember feeling your heartbeat
with my head
behind bookshelves

i remember the last time we hugged
your arms didn't wrap around the whole way

i should've known then
you were saying goodbye

the shoots

stoney brook

stoney brook travels alone
rapidly passing by
like my time at the house
my grandparents used to live in

i watched stoney brook from a rocking chair
on the deck my grandpa built

i caught my first crayfish in those waters
and i let it go

my grandpa's memory began to slip away
like the leaves and sticks
tumbling in the rapids

when he died
the house was sold
and i never saw the brook again

it was harder to let go that time

but i know that water runs deep
connects all lands

when i see a stream, a river, the sea
i remember stoney brook
and my grandpa

my body is a fireplace

a flame ignites inside my jack-o'-lantern head
my eyes and lips slits through which light escapes

when we kiss, our breaths mingle
fueling each others' fires

it starts on our tongues, singeing each taste bud
slides down our throats, settles in our hearts
the place for optimal damage

under the intense heat, my heart crinkles
like dry newspaper
explodes in a spark of yellow
reduced to black ash

but your heart is inflammable

ever since you lit me up and left
my eyes and ears are black with smoke
my chimney throat layered with your soot

i'm no longer looking for a fire starter
i need a chimney sweeper

sunset love

fallen sunset orange leaves
replaced by a blanket of snow

the willow tree we lay under
and took refuge in its shade

the big yellow adirondack chair
we snuggled on, feeling like giants
overlooking our kingdom

your soft artist's hand
a conduit carrying words to paper
your gift, your weapon

what we were
what i thought we were
the wind carelessly swept away

like the seasons
our colors changed
from sunrise yellow to supernova red

you cast away your beat-up sneakers
what good would they be in the snow

nonna's home

above the stop sign
where someone's long dark hair
mingled with fresh paint

next to the one-eyed cat
never blinking, always watching

to the right of bruised blackberries
oozing their sweet liquor
under the mediterranean sun

to the left of the red plastic chairs
where old men sit and play cards
women eagerly engage in gossip
teenagers stop and sip a beer

behind the curtains, pushed aside
by dough-covered hands
an apron splattered with tomato sauce

the directions to
my nonna's home

goodbye innocence

running to the swingset, our little legs stumbling
over the sandbox, you grabbed my hand
with your sticky sweet fingers, smelling of the
candy you'd stolen
whipped your head around, called out to my
parents: *you can go now*
because i was with you, king of the playground

ten years later
on a couch behind mummified bodies
sealed in an airtight glass case
you kissed me
breathing life through my parted lips

in a parked car next to the courts
i grew up on, playing tennis
i kissed you, but i didn't like it
when you put your hands on my head
pushed me down

i stayed under for a while
hidden, ashamed, safe

until i met you, and we danced in the dark
i wasn't afraid anymore
until you decided you didn't love me anymore

you'd rather sleep alone
keep your hands in your pockets

you didn't push me down, i fell
farther than before
you took a part of me
i can never have back

i'm here, waiting
for the giver
not the taker

i should have told you

i should have told you a long time ago
that i didn't like your voice, the way it quivered
when you were mad

i should have told you a long time ago
that my parents didn't like you
because they saw your demons

i should have told you a long time ago
i didn't like the ring you bought me
so tight i couldn't feel my finger
on our wedding day

i should have told you a long time ago
that i was sick of wearing turtlenecks
to cover the scars

i should have told you a long time ago
that i didn't want to have kids with you
because i would rather die than make you a father

i should have told you a long time ago
that i was leaving, for good
but i was afraid

i'm not afraid of you anymore
i'm terrified of living this life one more day

i should have told you a long time ago
but i'm telling you now:
goodbye

the Call

a great horned owl hoots
at dawn, its feathers concealed
by fog and pine needles

a chipmunk hears its Call
darts inside a rotting log

a dismembered limb
of a tree struck
by lightning

the wind sighs
through the hollow log
like a flute out of tune

a honey bee
on a dandelion
a flash of pollen

a caddisfly rebuilds
its home
with pebbles, toothpicks, pop tabs

gifts from a careless hiker
disposing of trash
in somebody's home

i hear it again
the Call

heard by my ancestors
when these woods were wild

i see their moonlit figures
in my corner of Earth

take me with you
i whisper

the figures retreat
deeper into the woods

i hear the Call
fainter now

i follow

Adam before Eve

she pulls me
to these beachfront mansions
glittering like sea glass

the sun here
never hidden by clouds

i wish i could wake
every morning to
her sighs

this is what Earth sounded like
before life existed

before whales crawled onto land
before man evolved hands
to build

these houses are but
stone she polished
and spit out

they belong to her
i stand before her

at dawn. before the early
risers and surfers

i am Adam
before Eve

just a man
and the sea

mother monarch

stripes of orange and black
not a speck
of stray paint

like how mother taught
me to stay inside the lines
of my coloring book

mother and i saw them
in August

if we were lucky.
before they flew
away

to a warmer place
maybe San Diego
or Mexico

their children
came back
to the milkweed mother
planted

when a sun's ray grazed
the underside of a leaf
mother pointed

at something milky
white, "there are caterpillars
inside" mother said

i could count on them
to be there
every year

one August
the monarchs stretched
their wings and flew
away with mother

i thought i'd never see her
again, but i do
every August

i watch her
get another chance at life

i watch her come home
and fly away
to places we could never
travel to

roller coaster

the creaking of an old wooden roller coaster
bound to break down
the screams of riders as they shot down the last hill
out of sight

every time they disappeared, i thought
they're not coming back
but sure enough they reappeared

it frightened me more than anything
because sometimes
people don't come back

i used to see the same people every thanksgiving
i could count on them to be there
but when grandpa died everything changed

seeing the chair where he used to sit
is like watching an empty seat
return on a roller coaster

 i rode the roller coaster for the first time
with my father

i clung to him, desperately trying
not to fly out of my seat

when our car came to a halt,
i smiled because we had made it
we had returned

i'm older now
and no longer afraid of rollercoasters

but every time my father leaves
i remember our roller coaster ride
and i wonder
what if he doesn't come back this time?

the runt

arms hanging over balconies
the scratch of wheels
on cobblestone streets

the smell of new things
and people from villages
with strange words

from my perch, cigarette
smoke creates a halo
around a pig
below

*papà, papà, i must
have that pig*

that one? he puffs
smoke in its
direction

past potted plants
and vendors, i run
to the pig

there he is
the runt

the days blur
like a setting mediterranean sun

and by Winter
he isn't a runt

too big, too round
for the wire home
papà made

i know what is coming

flecks of blood
on the doorstep
with the first snow

squeals and a silence
i can't bear

*papà, papà, what
have you done?*

you picked a good one
he drops the cigarette
to his heel, smiles

i go back to the
wire home
the imprint of my pig
in the hay

i lie there
until the smell of burning
wood and light of a fire
soak my eyelids

mamma and papà
pass a tray around
to upturned mouths
glowing in the firelight

secret garden

her heart is a secret garden
the walls are very high

only the eagles can reach
such heights, make nests
inside

concentric rose bushes
protect, hidden beneath
their red blooms

thorns are spindles
from spinning wheels

dark magic lies
on each silver tip

the sleeping victims
still upon the lawn

she surveys each one
with an unfeeling
stare

they are statues
carved for her

something white
protests

a letter
in a lifeless hand

her excited fingers
pry it out,
it's for her

true love can climb your walls
persevere through death
and any sleeping potion

but it cannot save
a heart
that does not want to be found

the loneliest place

the waves of the Atlantic
uncover sleeping sunbathers

two terns bob, hollow anchors
with eyes of beads
from broken friendship bracelets

white sun hats and umbrellas
a pale woman sips a margarita

sandy scalps and burned shoulders
of children, not hers

a crab scuttles between the pages
of her paperback, she brushes it
away

lovers kiss with salty lips
she tastes her salt-rimmed glass

a stray volleyball nudges her foot
she pushes it, flips a page

a father smears sunscreen
on his son's back, the places
he can't reach

she cranes her arm awkwardly
behind, misses a spot

this strip of sand
the loneliest place in the world

things i regret

not sharing my sandwich
with the kid with no lunch

laughing at a joke i thought was funny
but it hurt one of my best friends

not saying *i love you* to my dad before he died
drinking too much to try to forget

not letting my boyfriend tell me he loved me
because it wasn't the "right" moment

not traveling the world
because i didn't want to go alone

staring into the mirror
unhappy with the reflection

never swimming in the ocean
because i was sure i would drown

longing to have something worth regretting

black holes

yellow bus at the top of the hill
jammed legs, windows open
running through the woods
wavy lines on the horizon
sweaty bodies, melting popsicles

blue eyes cool like the ocean, the bottom of a pool
where i sink and hold
my breath in a black hole
the one the blue-eyed boy told me
to close my eyes, see the darkness
the light fluttering over my eyelids
retreating with each downward
stroke past the milky way to andromeda

hula-hoops spinning, friendship bracelets tied
around wrists, never to be cut off
summer sun slinking away
rubbing sound of tires coming
to a halt, smell of engine smoke
Lady Gaga's *Edge of Glory* brings me back
to Earth, the weight of gravity is mine
i slide the folded paper into his hands

step-two-three, step-two-three
one misstep, i'll step on his toes
my eyes dare an upward glance
to find rosy cheeks, a brace-filled smile
night creeps outside the windows, casts
long shadows, but we are bathed
in the chandelier's golden light

first love

i didn't know when i first met you
that you'd break my heart
like no one before

your bright blue eyes
seemingly calm on the surface
pulled me out, out, out to sea

your golden sunlit hair
reminds me of summer and our day by the pool
armed with water guns
(how clueless i was then of the weapons
you would use against me)

i miss the way you held me when i cried
the way you made me feel
like i was invincible as long as i had you
by my side

i will always remember the feeling
of your skin against mine
as we fell asleep, bodies entwined

you told me you weren't going
anywhere
and i foolishly believed you
gave you my heart
and more

i will always remember
how the first rays of dawn streaked across your face
like strokes of a paintbrush
as i woke up, realizing
you weren't a dream

but now
you are just a dream to me

museum

pages unturned by hands
yellowing on dusty bookshelves

pairs of shoes bought, never to touch
clacking heels muffled by tissue paper

a pen resting on stationary, uncapped
waiting to dance on paper
to transform scribbles to words

outside, the sun rises and sets
blinds seclude this still house

no light to reflect on empty photo frames
or grandfather's glasses, cracked
in grandmother's wrinkled hands

it was anything but still
the day before he died
and home became a museum

grandmother the marble statue

quarantine

like flower boxes in a greenhouse
we stand, separate
sprouting in our own soil

i wonder, will we hug again
will our stems intertwine
our petals glow
under the same sun

will we say hello to strangers
and invite friends into our homes

like birds of a flock
and a pod of dolphins
we are social animals

by the laws of nature
it is not wise
to stand alone

road to unknown

a white toothbrush crinkles in its wrapping
untouched from the outside world

a faded pair of blue jeans
seams ripping apart like my connection
to this house

yellow bricks hold stories from my past
a dirt road awaits, an escape route

i've waited long for this

one step forward in my laceless shoes
no strings attached

bare branches towering overhead
grasping at my loose hair in the wind
pulling me back to that pile of bricks

one step forward, not backward
that's where i'm headed

tipping forward, white toothbrush crinkling
a bag full of belongings settling
in the crook of my elbow

insignificant me wrapped
in the infinite dirt road

golden sun peeks through the turbulent sky
and i know
freedom awaits

storm clouds

fresh bread rising in the oven
a hand stained purple from blackberries plucked

a baby's blue eyes that never judge
no matter who i am

a hug i was afraid to ask for
but given nonetheless

there are so many people who love me
just because i am, i exist

when i run, i wonder at the cloudless sky
i don't notice the uneven sidewalk
tree roots struggling through the cement

i don't notice you
sitting on a paint-chipped park bench
asking why the world loves me
and hates you

why i can afford to ignore the uneven sidewalks
and oppressed tree roots reaching
for the same sunlight i bathe in

it's time to stop looking at the cloudless sky
and notice the storm clouds on the horizon

they've always been there
and they're not going away

thank you for reading this book!
i'd love to hear what you thought - you can email
me at:
snyderman.lucia@gmail.com

Printed in Great Britain
by Amazon